The Dopamine Drop

The Dopamine Drop

Suzanne Byrd

CONTENTS

1

Understanding the ADHD Brain in Perimenopause

For many women in their late 30s and 40s, a sudden and bewildering shift occurs. The mental strategies that once kept their ADHD symptoms in check begin to fail. Tasks that were manageable now feel insurmountable. Brain fog descends like a thick curtain, and forgetfulness becomes a daily frustration. Emotional regulation, already a challenge for many with ADHD, becomes even more unpredictable. At the same time, their bodies begin signaling the onset of perimenopause—hot flashes, irregular periods, and sleep disturbances. What few realize is that these two experiences are deeply intertwined.

This chapter explores the collision of ADHD and perimenopause, a phenomenon that leaves many women feeling like they're losing their minds. The truth is far more manageable—and far less frightening—than it seems. By understanding the biological mechanisms at play, women can reclaim agency over their cognitive and emotional well-being.

ADHD and Perimenopause: A Primer

ADHD is often misunderstood as a childhood condition, but for many women, diagnosis comes much later in life. Research shows a significant spike in ADHD diagnoses among women in their 30s and 40s, a period that also coincides with the onset of perimenopause. This timing is no coincidence.

Perimenopause, the transitional phase before menopause, is marked by fluctuating and eventually declining estrogen levels. These hormonal shifts affect nearly every system in the body, including the brain. For women with ADHD, whose brains already process dopamine differently, the drop in estrogen can feel like a sudden system failure.

ADHD is fundamentally a disorder of executive function—the brain's ability to plan, focus, regulate emotions, and recall information. Estrogen plays a critical role in modulating neurotransmitters like dopamine, which is essential for executive function. When estrogen levels fall, dopamine availability drops as well, exacerbating ADHD symptoms in ways that can feel alarming.

Estrogen's Role in Dopamine Regulation

Dopamine is often called the "motivation molecule" because it drives focus, reward-seeking behavior, and emotional regulation. In the ADHD brain, dopamine signaling is already impaired, making it harder to sustain attention and manage impulses. Estrogen acts as a dopamine regulator, enhancing its production and ensuring its efficient use in the brain.

Studies have shown that estrogen increases the density of dopamine receptors and boosts dopamine synthesis. When estrogen levels are stable, women with ADHD often find their symptoms more manageable. But during perimenopause, estrogen levels become erratic before declining sharply. This drop disrupts dopamine availability, leading to what many describe as a "crash"—a sudden worsening of ADHD symptoms.

For example, a woman who once relied on reminders and lists to stay organized may find these systems failing her. Tasks that required moderate effort now feel overwhelming. Emotional reactivity may spike, leaving her feeling like she's on an unpredictable rollercoaster. These changes are not a sign of personal failure or cognitive decline—they are the result of a neurochemical shift that can be understood and managed.

Why Symptoms Worsen: A Deep Dive

The intersection of ADHD and perimenopause manifests in several key symptoms, each tied to the drop in estrogen and its impact on dopamine.

Brain fog is one of the most common complaints. Women describe it as a mental haze, where thoughts feel sluggish and clarity is just out of reach. This occurs because dopamine is crucial for working memory—the brain's ability to hold and manipulate information in the moment. With less dopamine available, the brain struggles to process and retain information efficiently.

Forgetfulness also escalates. Misplacing keys, missing appointments, or walking into a room only to forget why—these lapses can be distressing. Again, dopamine plays a role in memory retrieval, and its depletion makes these moments more frequent.

Emotional dysregulation becomes more pronounced as well. The same dopamine pathways that govern focus also help regulate mood. When dopamine levels drop, emotional responses can become more intense and harder to control. A minor frustration might trigger disproportionate anger, or sadness may feel overwhelming without clear cause.

Differentiating ADHD from Early-Onset Dementia

One of the most frightening aspects of this hormonal and neurochemical shift is how closely it can mimic early-onset dementia. Women report fearing they're losing their cognitive abilities entirely, especially when forgetfulness and confusion become frequent. However, there are key differences between worsening ADHD symptoms and dementia.

ADHD-related memory lapses are typically situational—forgetting where you put your phone, struggling to recall a name, or losing track of a conversation. In contrast, dementia often involves more profound disorientation, such as forgetting how to perform familiar tasks or getting lost in well-known places.

Another distinction is that ADHD symptoms fluctuate. A woman might have days where her brain feels sharp and focused, followed by days where everything feels scattered. Dementia, on the other hand, tends to follow a steady decline without periods of improvement.

Tracking symptoms can provide clarity. Keeping a journal of memory lapses, mood swings, and focus challenges—along with menstrual cycle or perimenopausal symptoms—can reveal patterns tied to hormonal shifts rather than cognitive decline.

Practical Strategies for Managing the Crash

While the collision of ADHD and perimenopause can feel overwhelming, there are actionable steps to mitigate its impact.

Hormonal tracking is a powerful tool. Apps or journals that log menstrual cycles, mood changes, and cognitive symptoms can help identify correlations between estrogen fluctuations and ADHD symptom severity. This awareness alone can reduce anxiety, as it provides a concrete explanation for the changes.

Productivity tools may need an upgrade. As existing systems falter, experimenting with new strategies—such as voice memos for reminders, visual timers for task focus, or breaking tasks into smaller steps—can help compensate for dopamine-related challenges.

Lifestyle adjustments also play a critical role. Regular exercise, particularly aerobic activity, boosts dopamine production. A protein-rich diet supports neurotransmitter synthesis, and prioritizing sleep—though often difficult during perimenopause—helps stabilize cognitive function.

Finally, seeking professional support is key. A healthcare provider familiar with both ADHD and perimenopause can offer tailored interventions, whether through hormone therapy, ADHD medication adjustments, or therapeutic strategies for emotional regulation.

The "crash" that so many women experience is not a sign of irreversible decline—it's a neurochemical response to hormonal change. By understanding the interplay between estrogen and dopamine, women can reframe their symptoms not as personal failures, but as manageable fluctuations.

This chapter has laid the groundwork for recognizing and addressing the unique challenges of ADHD in perimenopause. The following chapters will build on this foundation, offering deeper dives into specific strategies for reclaiming focus, emotional balance, and confidence during this transitional phase. The journey isn't about fixing a broken brain—it's about adapting to its changing needs with compassion and knowledge.

2

The Science Behind the Crash

For many women in their late 30s and 40s, the sudden onset of forgetfulness, emotional turbulence, and mental fog can feel like an alarming personal failure. The to-do lists pile up, the misplaced keys multiply, and the frustration grows—yet no one seems to understand why. The truth is, this isn't a character flaw or the beginnings of cognitive decline. It's a neurological and hormonal shift, a collision of two powerful biological forces: ADHD and perimenopause.

This chapter will unravel the science behind what you're experiencing. We'll explore how estrogen and dopamine work together in the brain, why their disruption during perimenopause amplifies ADHD symptoms, and what recent research tells us about this often-overlooked intersection. By the end, you'll have a clearer understanding of the "crash"—and, most importantly, the reassurance that you're not imagining it.

The Hormone-Brain Connection

Estrogen does far more than regulate the reproductive system. It's a key player in brain function, influencing mood, memory, and cognitive clarity. One of its most critical roles is modulating dopamine, the neurotransmitter responsible for motivation, focus, and emotional regulation. Think of estrogen as a conductor, ensuring dopamine levels stay in harmony.

When perimenopause begins, estrogen levels fluctuate unpredictably before eventually declining. This instability disrupts dopamine production and signaling, leaving the ADHD brain—already prone to dopamine deficits—even more vulnerable. The result? Symptoms like brain fog, forgetfulness, and emotional dysregulation intensify.

For example, you might notice that tasks requiring sustained attention—like reading a report or following a conversation—suddenly feel impossible. Or perhaps minor frustrations now trigger overwhelming emotional reactions. These aren't signs of personal failure; they're the neurological ripple effects of hormone-mediated neurotransmitter imbalance.

Dopamine and Executive Function

Dopamine is often called the "motivation molecule," but its role extends far beyond getting things done. It's essential for executive function, the brain's command center for planning, decision-making, and impulse control. In ADHD, dopamine dysregulation is already a core challenge. When perimenopause further depletes dopamine, those challenges multiply.

Imagine trying to navigate a busy intersection with a traffic light that keeps flickering. That's what happens in the ADHD brain during perimenopause. Dopamine shortages disrupt signal clarity, making it harder to prioritize tasks, regulate emotions, or recall information.

Practical examples abound:

- You walk into a room and immediately forget why.
- Starting a project feels like climbing a mountain.

- Small setbacks provoke disproportionate frustration.

These aren't random lapses. They're the direct result of dopamine-starved neural pathways struggling to fire efficiently. Understanding this can help you reframe your experience—not as a personal shortcoming, but as a biological response.

ADHD Meets Perimenopause

The overlap of ADHD and perimenopause is a perfect storm, yet it's only recently gained attention in research. Studies now show that hormonal fluctuations can unmask or worsen ADHD symptoms in women who previously coped well. This explains why so many women receive their ADHD diagnosis in their 30s or 40s—right when perimenopause begins.

A common misconception is that these symptoms signal early-onset dementia. The fear is understandable: forgetting names, losing track of conversations, and struggling with routine tasks can be terrifying. But the root cause is different. Dementia involves neurodegeneration, while the perimenopausal ADHD crash stems from temporary neurotransmitter disruption.

Research also highlights a gender gap in ADHD diagnosis. Girls and women often present with inattentive-type ADHD, which is less disruptive but equally debilitating. Without the hyperactive stereotype, many go undiagnosed until hormonal shifts make their symptoms impossible to ignore.

The Crash Explained

So, what exactly is the "crash"? It's the sudden, often bewildering exacerbation of ADHD symptoms triggered by perimenopausal hormone fluctuations. Here's how it unfolds:

1. Estrogen levels drop, reducing dopamine availability.
2. The ADHD brain, already dopamine-sensitive, struggles to compensate.
3. Executive functions—focus, memory, emotional control—start to falter.
4. Stress increases, further depleting dopamine and creating a vicious cycle.

This crash isn't permanent, but it is physiological. Recognizing it as a biological response, not a personal failing, is the first step toward managing it effectively.

The Research Landscape

Recent studies are finally shedding light on the ADHD-perimenopause connection. A 2022 study in The Journal of Clinical Endocrinology & Metabolism found that women with ADHD reported significantly worse symptoms during perimenopause compared to those without ADHD. Another study highlighted that estrogen therapy could mitigate some cognitive symptoms, suggesting a direct hormonal link.

However, gaps remain. Most ADHD research has focused on men and children, leaving women—especially midlife women—understudied. More investigation is needed into tailored treatments, such as hormone therapy's role in managing ADHD symptoms during perimenopause.

For readers eager to dive deeper, resources like the Journal of Women's Health and the ADHD and Perimenopause Research Initiative offer valuable insights.

Bringing It All Together

If this chapter resonates with you, take a deep breath. What you're experiencing has a name, a cause, and a growing body of research behind it. The crash isn't your fault—it's a collision of biology and timing.

Armed with this knowledge, you can start to reframe your struggles. Those forgotten appointments? They're not carelessness. The emotional rollercoaster? It's not instability. They're signs of a brain adapting to hormonal change.

In the chapters ahead, we'll explore strategies to navigate this phase—from lifestyle adjustments to medical interventions. For now, let this understanding settle in: You're not broken. You're navigating a complex, underrecognized transition with resilience. And that, in itself, is something to celebrate.

3

Recognizing the Signs

For years, you've managed your ADHD symptoms with relative success—until suddenly, everything feels harder. The mental fog thickens. The keys vanish not just once, but three times before breakfast. The emotional turbulence leaves you reeling, wondering if you're losing your grip. If this sounds familiar, you're not alone. Women in their 30s and 40s are experiencing a surge in ADHD diagnoses, coinciding with the onset of perimenopause. But here's the critical link: estrogen, the hormone that helps regulate dopamine, begins its decline during this phase. When estrogen drops, dopamine regulation falters, and ADHD symptoms intensify. What many women mistake for early-onset dementia or a personal failing is often the collision of ADHD and perimenopause—a phenomenon we call "the crash."

This chapter is your guide to recognizing these symptoms for what they truly are. We'll explore the hormonal science behind the crash, identify the most common (and commonly misunderstood) symptoms, and differentiate ADHD exacerbations from other conditions. Most importantly, you'll find actionable strategies and real-life stories to help you navigate this turbulent phase with clarity and confidence.

Understanding the Hormonal Impact

Estrogen isn't just a reproductive hormone; it's a neuroregulator. It enhances dopamine production and receptor sensitivity, two factors critical for focus, motivation, and emotional stability. For women with ADHD, whose brains already struggle with dopamine efficiency, the perimenopausal estrogen drop can feel like losing a lifeline.

Research shows that estrogen fluctuations directly impact executive function. A 2022 study in Menopause found that women with ADHD reported a 40% increase in symptom severity during perimenopause compared to their premenopausal baseline. Imagine your brain's dopamine supply as a reservoir. Pre-perimenopause, estrogen helps keep it adequately filled. As estrogen declines, the reservoir drains, leaving ADHD symptoms to surge.

Practical examples abound. Sarah, a 42-year-old project manager, noticed her once-reliable organizational systems failing. "I'd set calendar alerts and still miss meetings. My brain felt like a browser with 50 tabs open—none of them loading." Another woman, Priya, described crying over minor frustrations, something she'd never done before. "I wondered if I was depressed, but my therapist pointed out my ADHD meds weren't working like they used to." These stories underscore a vital truth: what's happening isn't personal failure or dementia. It's biology.

Common Symptoms and Their Misinterpretations

The crash manifests in ways that often masquerade as other conditions. Brain fog, for instance, is frequently mistaken for early dementia. Forgetfulness escalates beyond typical ADHD lapses—you might blank on your best friend's name or leave the stove on overnight. Emotional dysregulation can mimic mood disorders, with outbursts or tearfulness that seem disproportionate to the trigger.

Take Maria, a nurse who prided herself on her composure. "I snapped at a patient for asking a routine question. Later, I sobbed in my car, horrified at myself." She feared she was developing a personality disorder until her doctor connected the dots to her plummeting estrogen levels. Similarly, brain fog is often mislabeled as "menopause brain," but for ADHD women, it's more debilitating. Tasks that required minimal effort now demand Herculean focus.

Key distinctions exist. Dementia-related memory loss typically involves forgetting entire experiences, not just details. ADHD forgetfulness is more situational—losing track of conversations mid-sentence, not recalling whether you took your vitamins. Mood swings from perimenopause alone lack the ADHD hallmark of rejection-sensitive dysphoria, that visceral reaction to perceived criticism. Recognizing these nuances is the first step toward accurate self-assessment.

Differentiating ADHD from Other Conditions

The overlap between ADHD exacerbations, depression, anxiety, and dementia can be confounding. Depression often saps motivation uniformly, while ADHD-related inertia is task-specific (e.g., unable to start taxes but hyperfocusing on a hobby). Anxiety may cause racing thoughts, but ADHD's are more disjointed—jumping from "I need milk" to "What if my cat hates me?" in seconds.

Clinical tools can help. The Barkley Adult ADHD Rating Scale includes perimenopause-specific questions, such as whether symptoms worsened in tandem with menstrual irregularity. Tracking symptom patterns across your cycle is invaluable. If focus plummets during low-estrogen phases (like the week before your period), it's a strong indicator of hormonal influence.

Consulting a healthcare provider is crucial, but come prepared. Describe not just symptoms but their contexts: "I forget appointments more often in the two weeks before my period." Request hormone level checks alongside ADHD assessments. Misdiagnosis is common—one study found 30% of perimenopausal women with ADHD were initially treated for depression alone—so advocate for comprehensive evaluation.

Personal Anecdotes and Case Studies

Real stories illuminate the path forward. Lisa, a teacher, thought she was "losing her mind" when she mixed up her students' names daily. "I'd taught for 15 years—this wasn't me." Hormone therapy combined with adjusted ADHD medication restored her clarity. Then there's Naomi, who attributed her exhaustion to aging until she tracked her symptoms and noticed they spiked during estrogen dips. Simple interventions—protein-rich snacks, midday walks—eased the crashes.

These women's experiences reveal universal truths: symptom tracking is empowering, and small adjustments yield outsized gains. Their journeys also normalize the shame many feel. "I blamed myself for being lazy," admits Rachel, a lawyer. "Learning this was hormonal let me stop the self-punishment."

Actionable Strategies for Symptom Management

Knowledge is power, but action is liberation. Start by syncing your ADHD strategies with your hormonal cycle. During low-estrogen phases, simplify tasks: use voice memos instead of lists, or delegate high-focus work. Body doubling—having a companion nearby while you work—can combat inertia.

Nutrition matters. Dopamine production requires tyrosine, found in eggs, lean meats, and almonds. Pair these with complex carbs to stabilize blood sugar, which dips with estrogen. Exercise, even a 10-minute walk, boosts dopamine and clears brain fog.

For emotional dysregulation, practice "pause and reflect." When overwhelmed, ask: "Is this emotion proportional, or is my ADHD brain amplifying it?" Cognitive behavioral techniques, like reframing thoughts ("I forgot again, but it's my hormones, not my worth"), help too.

The crash is disorienting, but it's not a life sentence. By recognizing the signs as hormonal-ADHD interplay—not dementia or personal failure—you reclaim agency. Track your patterns, adapt your strategies, and seek support. Perimenopause may amplify ADHD, but it also unveils your resilience. The women in these pages didn't just survive their crashes; they learned to navigate them with grace. You can too.

Remember: this isn't your brain breaking. It's your body signaling for new tools. The next chapter will explore those tools in depth—turning insight into action.

4

Hormonal Tracking and Its Benefits

For women navigating the complex intersection of ADHD and perimenopause, understanding the nuances of hormonal fluctuations can feel like deciphering a foreign language. The sudden onset of brain fog, forgetfulness, and emotional turbulence can be disorienting, even alarming. Many women find themselves wondering if they are developing early-onset dementia, only to discover that what they are experiencing is a hormonal "crash." The key to managing this lies in hormonal tracking—a proactive, empowering tool that provides clarity and control during a time of uncertainty.

Introduction to Hormonal Tracking

Hormonal tracking is more than just a buzzword; it is a lifeline for women with ADHD who are grappling with the onset of perimenopause. At its core, hormonal tracking involves monitoring changes in hormone levels, particularly estrogen, to understand their impact on physical and cognitive function. For women with ADHD, this practice is especially vital because estrogen plays a critical role in dopamine regulation—the neurotransmitter responsible for focus, motivation, and emotional stability.

When estrogen levels fluctuate or decline during perimenopause, dopamine production is disrupted, leading to exacerbated ADHD symptoms. Brain fog becomes more pervasive, forgetfulness more frequent, and emotional dysregulation more intense. By tracking hormonal changes, women can identify patterns and correlations between their hormone levels and ADHD symptoms, gaining valuable insights into their body's unique rhythms.

Hormonal tracking is not just about collecting data; it is about fostering a deeper connection with your body and brain. It empowers you to anticipate challenges, make informed decisions, and take proactive steps to mitigate the impact of hormonal fluctuations on your daily life. In a world where ADHD and perimenopause often feel like uncharted territory, hormonal tracking offers a roadmap to greater clarity and control.

Tools and Methods for Hormonal Tracking

There is no one-size-fits-all approach to hormonal tracking. Fortunately, a variety of tools and methods are available, catering to different preferences and lifestyles. Whether you are tech-savvy or prefer a more hands-on approach, there is a tracking method that suits your needs.

Mobile apps have become increasingly popular for hormonal tracking, offering convenience and accessibility. Apps like Clue, Flo, and Hormonify allow users to log symptoms, menstrual cycles, and mood changes, often providing predictive analytics based on historical data. These apps can be particularly useful for identifying patterns over time, such as recurring brain fog or emotional instability.

Wearable devices, such as Fitbit and Apple Watch, also offer hormonal tracking features, integrating data on sleep, activity, and heart rate to provide a holistic view of your health. Some devices even measure metrics like skin temperature and heart rate variability, which can offer additional insights into hormonal changes.

For those who prefer a more manual approach, journaling remains a reliable and effective method. A simple notebook or planner can be used to record daily symptoms, mood changes, and energy levels. This method encourages mindfulness and self-reflection, allowing you to tune into your body's signals without relying on technology.

When choosing a tracking tool, consider your lifestyle, goals, and comfort level with technology. If you prefer simplicity, a paper journal might be the best option. If you value data analysis and predictive insights, a mobile app or wearable device may be more suitable. The key is to choose a method that feels sustainable and intuitive for you.

Practical Application of Hormonal Tracking

The true power of hormonal tracking lies in its practical application. Once you have collected data, the next step is to interpret it and use it to inform your daily life. This process involves identifying patterns, making connections, and adjusting your routines to align with your body's needs.

Start by reviewing your tracked data regularly, looking for recurring symptoms or trends. For example, you may notice that brain fog tends to intensify during the luteal phase of your menstrual cycle, when estrogen levels are lower. Or you might find that emotional dysregulation peaks during periods of stress or poor sleep. By pinpointing these patterns, you can anticipate challenges and plan accordingly.

Once you have identified patterns, consider how they intersect with your ADHD symptoms. For instance, if you know that low estrogen levels exacerbate your forgetfulness, you might schedule important tasks or meetings during periods when estrogen is higher. Similarly, if you notice that fatigue and brain fog are more pronounced in the afternoon, you could prioritize morning hours for tasks that require focus and concentration.

Hormonal tracking also offers valuable insights into self-care and lifestyle adjustments. If you observe that certain foods or activities worsen your symptoms, you can experiment with alternatives to see what works best for you. For example, some women find that reducing caffeine intake or incorporating mindfulness practices like meditation helps stabilize mood and energy levels.

Remember, hormonal tracking is a dynamic process. It requires patience, curiosity, and a willingness to adapt. As you continue to collect data and refine your approach, you will gain a deeper understanding of your body's unique rhythms and how to work with them, rather than against them.

Predicting and Managing Brain Offline Periods

One of the most tangible benefits of hormonal tracking is its ability to help you predict and manage "brain offline" periods—those times when your cognitive function feels sluggish, and ADHD symptoms are at their peak. By anticipating these periods, you can take proactive steps to minimize their impact on your productivity and well-being.

Begin by using your tracked data to identify when brain offline periods are most likely to occur. For many women, these periods coincide with specific phases of the menstrual cycle or times of hormonal fluctuation. Once you have pinpointed these windows, you can plan your schedule around them.

For example, if you know that brain fog tends to strike in the days leading up to your period, you might avoid scheduling high-stakes meetings or deadlines during that time. Instead, use those days for tasks that require less cognitive effort, such as organizing, filing, or brainstorming creatively.

It's also helpful to establish self-care rituals during brain offline periods. This might include prioritizing rest, engaging in gentle physical activity like yoga or walking, and practicing mindfulness techniques to soothe emotional dysregulation. Consider setting reminders to hydrate, eat nutritious meals, and take breaks throughout the day to recharge.

In some cases, you may need to communicate your needs to others. If you have a supportive partner, family member, or coworker, let them know when you anticipate a brain offline period and how they can help. This might mean delegating tasks, asking for understanding, or simply creating a quieter, less demanding environment during those times.

The goal is not to eliminate brain offline periods entirely—that's rarely possible—but to navigate them with grace and self-compassion. By planning ahead and adjusting your expectations, you can reduce their impact on your productivity and mental well-being.

Common Pitfalls and Mistakes to Avoid

As with any new practice, hormonal tracking comes with its share of potential pitfalls. Being aware of these common mistakes can help you sidestep them and ensure that your tracking efforts are effective and sustainable.

One common mistake is inconsistency. Tracking works best when it's done regularly, so aim to make it a daily habit. Set reminders or integrate tracking into your existing routines, such as logging symptoms while brushing your teeth or reviewing data during your morning coffee.

Another pitfall is overanalyzing. While it's important to look for patterns, avoid fixating on every fluctuation or outlier. Hormonal changes are complex and influenced by a variety of factors, from stress to diet to environmental triggers. Focus on overarching trends rather than isolated data points.

It's also easy to fall into the trap of perfectionism. Remember, hormonal tracking is not about achieving flawless data; it's about gaining insights and making informed decisions. If you miss a day or forget to log a symptom, don't stress. Simply pick up where you left off and keep moving forward.

Finally, avoid relying solely on technology. While apps and wearable devices are valuable tools, they are not a substitute for your own intuition and self-awareness. Use technology as a supplement, not a replacement, for tuning into your body's signals.

Hormonal tracking is more than a practical tool—it is a transformative practice that empowers women with ADHD to navigate the challenges of perimenopause with confidence and clarity. By understanding the connection between estrogen and dopamine, and by using tracking methods to identify patterns and predict brain offline periods, you can take control of your symptoms and reclaim your mental well-being.

It's important to remember that hormonal tracking is a journey, not a destination. It requires patience, curiosity, and a willingness to adapt. As you continue to refine your approach, you will discover new insights into your body and brain, allowing you to make informed decisions that support your health and happiness.

In a world where ADHD and perimenopause can feel overwhelming, hormonal tracking offers a beacon of hope. It reminds us that we are not at the mercy of our hormones or our ADHD—we have the power to understand, anticipate, and manage their impact. By embracing this practice, you can navigate the "crash" with resilience and emerge stronger, more empowered, and more in tune with yourself than ever before.

5

Neuro-Affirming Productivity Strategies

Navigating the complexities of ADHD during perimenopause can feel like trying to solve a puzzle with constantly shifting pieces. As estrogen levels decline, dopamine regulation falters, exacerbating ADHD symptoms and leaving many women feeling overwhelmed, forgetful, and emotionally dysregulated. It's easy to fall into the trap of self-criticism, blaming yourself for what feels like a sudden inability to function. But what if the solution lies not in fighting against your brain's wiring but in embracing it? This chapter explores neuro-affirming productivity strategies—practical, compassionate approaches designed to work with your ADHD brain rather than against it. By understanding and implementing these techniques, you can reclaim your focus, reduce overwhelm, and navigate this challenging phase with greater ease.

What Are Neuro-Affirming Strategies?

Neuro-affirming strategies are rooted in the principle of self-acceptance and respect for neurodivergence. Instead of viewing ADHD as a deficit that needs fixing, these strategies emphasize working with your brain's unique strengths and challenges. For women in perimenopause, this approach is particularly crucial. The hormonal fluctuations that accompany this life stage can amplify ADHD symptoms, making traditional productivity methods feel impossible. Neuro-affirming practices offer a gentler, more sustainable way forward.

At their core, neuro-affirming strategies prioritize self-compassion. This means letting go of the expectation that you should function like someone without ADHD and instead embracing tools and techniques tailored to your brain's needs. For example, instead of berating yourself for forgetting an important task, you might focus on creating systems that reduce reliance on memory, such as visual aids or reminders. Similarly, rather than forcing yourself to work in ways that feel unnatural or exhausting, you might explore methods that align with your natural rhythms and energy levels.

The benefits of neuro-affirming strategies extend beyond productivity. By reducing the pressure to conform to neurotypical standards, you can lower stress levels and improve your overall well-being. This, in turn, creates a positive feedback loop: As you feel less overwhelmed, your ability to focus and stay organized improves. Embracing this mindset is not just a productivity hack—it's a form of self-care.

The Power of Lists and Visual Aids

One of the most effective neuro-affirming strategies is the use of lists and visual aids. For the ADHD brain, mental clutter can feel like a fog that obscures even the simplest tasks. Writing things down or creating visual representations of your responsibilities can cut through this fog, providing clarity and reducing overwhelm.

Lists are particularly powerful because they externalize your thoughts, freeing up mental space. However, not all lists are created equal. A sprawling, unstructured to-do list can feel just as overwhelming as the tasks themselves. Instead, try creating focused, prioritized lists. Break tasks into smaller, manageable steps and assign priorities based on urgency or importance. For example, instead of writing "Clean the house," break it down into "Vacuum the living room," "Wipe down the kitchen counter," and "Organize the bathroom cabinet." This approach makes tasks feel less daunting and provides a clear roadmap for your day.

Visual aids, such as calendars, color-coded systems, or sticky notes, can also be incredibly helpful. These tools provide a tangible representation of time and tasks, making it easier to stay on track. For instance, a wall calendar with color-coded categories for work, personal, and family commitments can give you a quick overview of your week. Posting sticky notes with reminders in visible locations can help you remember important tasks without relying on your memory.

Real-world examples illustrate the effectiveness of these strategies. Consider Sarah, a 42-year-old graphic designer who struggled with forgetfulness and overwhelm during perimenopause. By switching from a cluttered to-do list to a prioritized, step-by-step system, she found herself completing tasks more efficiently and with less stress. Similarly, Maria, a 38-year-old teacher, used a color-coded calendar to manage her work and personal life, finding that the visual representation helped her stay organized and focused. These tools are not one-size-fits-all, but experimenting with different formats can help you find what works best for your brain.

Body Doubling: A Game-Changer for Focus and Accountability

Another neuro-affirming strategy that has gained traction in the ADHD community is body doubling. This technique involves having another person present—physically or virtually—while you work on a task. The presence of the other person creates a sense of accountability and helps you stay focused, even if they are not directly involved in your task.

The concept of body doubling may sound simple, but its impact can be profound. For many women with ADHD, the challenge isn't knowing what to do—it's getting started or staying on task. The presence of another person can provide the external motivation needed to overcome this hurdle. Whether it's a friend sitting quietly in the same room or a virtual study buddy on a video call, body doubling can help you stay engaged and productive.

Finding a body double doesn't have to be complicated. Start by identifying tasks that feel particularly challenging or overwhelming. Then, reach out to a trusted friend or family member who is willing to spend time with you while you work. If in-person options are limited, consider joining an online body doubling community or scheduling virtual sessions with a colleague. The key is to find someone who understands your needs and can provide the right level of support.

Real-world success stories highlight the effectiveness of body doubling. For example, Lisa, a 45-year-old writer, struggled with procrastination and self-doubt during perimenopause. By scheduling weekly body doubling sessions with a fellow writer, she found herself completing projects more consistently and with greater confidence. Similarly, Rachel, a 39-year-old entrepreneur, used virtual body doubling to tackle administrative tasks, finding that the presence of her colleague helped her stay focused and motivated. These examples demonstrate how a simple strategy can yield powerful results.

Combining Strategies with Hormonal Tracking

While neuro-affirming strategies can be transformative on their own, their effectiveness can be enhanced by integrating them with hormonal tracking. Perimenopause is marked by significant hormonal fluctuations, and understanding these patterns can help you predict and manage executive function crashes.

Hormonal tracking involves monitoring your cycle and identifying times when your estrogen levels are likely to dip. These low-estrogen phases often correlate with increased ADHD symptoms, such as brain fog, emotional dysregulation, and forgetfulness. By tracking your hormones, you can anticipate these challenging periods and adjust your productivity strategies accordingly.

There are several ways to track your hormones, ranging from apps to journals. Apps like Flo, Clue, or Hormonology can help you log symptoms and identify patterns. Alternatively, you might prefer a traditional journal, where you can note your mood, energy levels, and productivity each day. The key is to find a method that feels intuitive and sustainable.

Once you've identified your hormonal patterns, you can tailor your neuro-affirming strategies to align with your cycle. For example, during high-estrogen phases, you might focus on tackling complex tasks or starting new projects. During low-estrogen phases, you might prioritize simpler, maintenance-oriented tasks or schedule extra body doubling sessions. This approach allows you to work with your body's natural rhythms rather than fighting against them.

Real-world examples illustrate the power of combining hormonal tracking with neuro-affirming strategies. For instance, Emma, a 40-year-old photographer, used a hormone-tracking app to identify her cycle's low points. During these times, she adjusted her schedule to focus on editing photos—a task that felt manageable even when her energy was low. Similarly, Jessica, a 43-year-old nurse, used hormonal tracking to plan her body doubling sessions, finding that this combination helped her stay productive even during challenging weeks. These examples demonstrate how small adjustments can make a big difference.

Navigating ADHD during perimenopause doesn't have to feel like an insurmountable challenge. By embracing neuro-affirming strategies, you can work with your brain's unique wiring rather than against it. Lists and visual aids can cut through mental clutter, providing clarity and reducing overwhelm. Body doubling can offer the accountability and focus needed to tackle challenging tasks. Combining these strategies with hormonal tracking allows you to anticipate and manage executive function crashes with greater ease.

Above all, remember that this process is about self-compassion and acceptance. You are not broken, and you are not failing. You are navigating a complex and often misunderstood phase of life with resilience and grace. By adopting these neuro-affirming strategies, you can reclaim your focus, reduce stress, and move through perimenopause with confidence and clarity.

6

Creating Your Personalized Plan

If you've made it this far, you've likely recognized that your ADHD symptoms have intensified during perimenopause—and you're not imagining it. The hormonal shifts of this life stage directly impact dopamine regulation, leaving you feeling like your brain is working against you. But here's the good news: You don't have to resign yourself to the chaos. This chapter will guide you through crafting a personalized plan that aligns with your unique neurobiology, hormonal fluctuations, and daily demands.

Understanding Your Unique Needs

Before you can build an effective strategy, you need clarity on how ADHD and perimenopause intersect in your life. Start by identifying your most disruptive symptoms. Are you struggling with forgetfulness? Emotional dysregulation? Crippling brain fog? These challenges likely fluctuate with your hormonal cycle, meaning they aren't static—and neither should your solutions be.

Begin with a two-week self-assessment. Track symptoms alongside energy levels, focus, and mood. Use a simple journal or an app designed for ADHD or cycle tracking (like Clue or Bearable). Note patterns: Do you lose your keys more often in the week before your period? Does your motivation plummet during ovulation? This isn't about judgment; it's about gathering data to work with your brain, not against it.

For example, Sarah, a 42-year-old graphic designer, realized her emotional outbursts coincided with her luteal phase. Once she recognized this pattern, she scheduled high-stakes client meetings for her follicular phase (when estrogen rises) and reserved administrative tasks for her lower-energy days. Awareness alone reduced her shame—and helped her plan proactively.

Integrating Hormonal Tracking

Hormones aren't the enemy; they're information. Estrogen, which boosts dopamine activity, declines unevenly during perimenopause. Tracking these shifts helps you anticipate—and mitigate—symptom flare-ups.

Start by charting your cycle, even if it's irregular. Note physical cues (breast tenderness, sleep changes) alongside cognitive ones (memory lapses, impulsivity). Over time, you'll identify your personal "danger zones"—phases where ADHD symptoms peak—and your "power phases," when focus comes more easily.

Pair this with a productivity audit. When are you most alert? Most distractible? For instance, if you're sharper in the mornings but hormonally foggy post-lunch, protect that morning window for deep work. Use afternoons for low-stakes tasks like emails or laundry. Tools like hormone-tracking apps can overlay symptom data with your calendar, creating a visual roadmap of your month.

Neuro-Affirming Productivity Strategies

Traditional productivity advice often fails neurodivergent brains. Instead of forcing yourself into rigid systems, adapt strategies that honor your wiring.

Visual aids are your allies. A whiteboard with priority tasks (color-coded by urgency) can bypass working memory deficits. Digital tools like Trello or Notion allow you to organize projects in a way that feels engaging, not overwhelming.

Body doubling—working alongside someone else, even virtually—can combat task paralysis. Join a Zoom co-working session or invite a friend to tackle chores together. The external accountability bridges the motivation gap when dopamine is scarce.

For example, Mia, a writer with ADHD, used to berate herself for abandoning half-finished drafts. Then she created a "scraps folder" where she could dump disjointed ideas without pressure. Later, during her high-energy phase, she'd revisit them. This small shift reduced her perfectionism and increased output.

Setting Realistic Goals

Ambition isn't the problem; unrealistic expectations are. Perimenopause + ADHD means some days, "success" might look like showering and eating lunch. That's okay.

Use the SMART framework—but adapt it for your brain. Instead of "I'll clean the entire house," try "I'll declutter one shelf today." Break goals into micro-tasks: "Open laptop" → "Write one sentence" → "Celebrate." Tiny wins build momentum.

Prioritize tasks based on your hormonal phase. Save complex decisions for high-estrogen days. During low phases, focus on maintenance: hydration, gentle movement, and saying no to non-essential demands.

Consider Lisa, a nurse who beat herself up for forgetting medication doses. She started placing pills next to her toothbrush—a habit stack that required no extra memory. Small, sustainable tweaks like this compound over time.

Building Your Personalized Plan

Now, synthesize what you've learned. Create a flexible template that accounts for:

1. Your symptom patterns (from tracking)
2. Your productivity rhythms (peak times, energy dips)
3. Your non-negotiables (sleep, nutrition, movement)

Experiment and iterate. Try blocking out "focus bursts" of 25 minutes followed by breaks. Test alarm reminders for medication or meals. If a strategy fails, tweak it—don't discard it.

Finally, build a support system. Share your plan with a trusted friend or therapist. Join communities of women navigating similar challenges (online forums like Perimenopause Hub or ADHD Reddit threads). You're not failing; you're adapting.

Perimenopause and ADHD can feel like a perfect storm, but you're the captain of this ship. By understanding your unique needs, tracking hormonal impacts, and implementing neuro-affirming strategies, you're not just surviving—you're rewriting the narrative. Progress isn't linear. Some days will be harder, and that's normal. Celebrate the small victories. You're not broken; you're evolving. And with this personalized plan, you're equipped to meet yourself where you are—with compassion and clarity.

The next chapter will explore long-term sustainability: how to adjust your plan as your body changes, and when to seek professional support.

But for now, take a breath. You've already done the hardest part: starting.

7

Managing Brain Fog and Forgetfulness

The moment you walk into a room and forget why you came in. The frustration of losing your train of thought mid-sentence. The sinking feeling when you miss an important deadline—again. If these experiences have become more frequent in your 30s or 40s, you're not alone. For women with ADHD, perimenopause can feel like a cognitive betrayal, as brain fog and forgetfulness intensify seemingly overnight. But here's the crucial truth: you are not losing your mind, and you are not developing dementia. You are experiencing what I call the "crash"—a collision of hormonal shifts and neurochemical changes that disrupt an already delicate balance in the ADHD brain.

This chapter will guide you through understanding why this happens and, more importantly, how to reclaim clarity and control. We'll explore the science behind the crash, practical daily strategies, memory-boosting techniques, and inspiring stories from women who've navigated this phase successfully. By the end, you'll have a personalized action plan to manage these symptoms with confidence.

The Science Behind the Crash

To understand why brain fog and forgetfulness worsen during perimenopause, we need to examine the relationship between estrogen and dopamine. Estrogen, a hormone that fluctuates and declines during perimenopause, plays a critical role in regulating dopamine—the neurotransmitter central to focus, motivation, and memory. For women with ADHD, whose brains already struggle with dopamine regulation, this drop can feel catastrophic.

Recent studies have shown that estrogen enhances dopamine receptor sensitivity and availability in key brain regions like the prefrontal cortex, which governs executive function. When estrogen levels dip, so does dopamine efficiency, exacerbating ADHD symptoms. This hormonal shift explains why tasks that once felt manageable now seem insurmountable, and why forgetfulness becomes more pronounced.

It's essential to recognize that these cognitive changes are not a sign of permanent decline. Research confirms that while perimenopausal brain fog is real, it is also temporary and manageable. By addressing the root causes—hormonal fluctuations and dopamine depletion—you can mitigate their impact and restore cognitive function.

Practical Tips for Daily Management

Living with brain fog and forgetfulness requires a shift in strategy. The key is to work with your brain, not against it. Here are some evidence-based techniques to help you navigate daily challenges:

First, break tasks into smaller, more manageable steps. Large projects can feel overwhelming, especially when focus is elusive. Instead of writing "clean the house," try "vacuum the living room" or "wipe down the kitchen counters." Completing these micro-tasks provides a sense of accomplishment and reduces mental fatigue.

Second, leverage external reminders. Alarms, sticky notes, and digital alerts can compensate for memory lapses. Set reminders for everything—taking medication, starting dinner, or even pausing to drink water. Technology can be a powerful ally; apps like Todoist or Google Keep allow you to offload mental clutter onto a reliable system.

Third, prioritize hydration, nutrition, and sleep. Dehydration worsens cognitive function, so keep a water bottle handy. Incorporate protein-rich snacks and omega-3 fatty acids to support brain health. And don't underestimate sleep—poor sleep exacerbates ADHD symptoms, so establish a calming bedtime routine to improve rest quality.

Finally, maintain consistency where possible. A predictable daily structure reduces decision fatigue and frees up mental energy for unexpected challenges. Even small routines, like a morning checklist or an evening wind-down ritual, can create stability in an otherwise foggy brain.

Memory Aids and Techniques

When your memory feels unreliable, external tools and techniques can bridge the gap. Visual aids, for example, tap into the ADHD brain's strength in visual processing. Use color-coded calendars, whiteboards, or even post-it notes in high-traffic areas to keep important information front and center.

Body doubling—working alongside another person—can also enhance focus and accountability. Whether it's a coworker, friend, or virtual study buddy, having someone nearby can reduce procrastination and improve task completion.

Chunking information is another effective strategy. Instead of trying to remember a long list, group items into categories. For instance, grocery lists can be divided by department (produce, dairy, pantry), making them easier to recall.

Technology offers a wealth of memory aids. Digital planners like Notion or Trello help organize tasks and deadlines, while voice memo apps allow you to capture thoughts on the go. For those who prefer analog methods, bullet journaling combines creativity with structure, providing a tactile way to track responsibilities.

Mindfulness and meditation can also improve memory retention. Even five minutes of daily practice can strengthen focus and reduce mental clutter. Apps like Headspace or Insight Timer offer guided sessions tailored to beginners, making mindfulness accessible despite a busy schedule.

Case Studies: Stories of Success

Real-world examples can offer hope and practical insights. Meet Laura, a 42-year-old graphic designer who struggled with forgetfulness during perimenopause. She began using a combination of digital reminders and a bullet journal, which helped her track deadlines and hormonal cycles. By noticing patterns in her cognitive dips, she could plan demanding tasks during her more focused days.

Then there's Priya, a teacher who felt her brain fog was sabotaging her career. She introduced protein-rich breakfasts and midday walks, which stabilized her energy and mental clarity. She also started body doubling with a colleague during grading sessions, turning a dreaded task into a social, productive activity.

These women's stories highlight a common thread: success came from experimentation and self-compassion. There is no one-size-fits-all solution, but by trying different strategies and honoring their unique needs, they found ways to thrive.

Building a Personalized Action Plan

Now it's your turn. Start by identifying your biggest challenges—perhaps it's forgetting appointments or losing focus during meetings. Then, select one or two strategies from this chapter to implement. Track your progress for a few weeks, noting what works and what doesn't.

Incorporate hormonal tracking if you haven't already. Apps like Clue or Flo can help you recognize patterns in your cognitive symptoms relative to your cycle. This awareness allows you to anticipate tough days and adjust your schedule accordingly.

Finally, cultivate resilience. There will be setbacks, and that's okay. ADHD and perimenopause require adaptability, not perfection. Celebrate small wins, seek support when needed, and remember that this phase is temporary.

Brain fog and forgetfulness during perimenopause can feel isolating, but they are not a life sentence. By understanding the science behind the crash, adopting practical strategies, and learning from others' experiences, you can navigate this transition with greater ease. Your brain is not broken—it's adapting. With the right tools and self-compassion, you can reclaim your clarity and confidence, one step at a time.

8

: Emotional Regulation During Hormonal Shifts

The intersection of ADHD and perimenopause is a perfect storm of biological and neurological challenges. For women navigating this transition, emotional regulation can feel like trying to hold water in cupped hands—no matter how tightly you squeeze, it slips through. The sudden mood swings, irritability, and overwhelming emotional responses aren't a personal failing. They're the result of a hormonal shift that directly impacts brain chemistry. This chapter will guide you through understanding why these changes occur and how to regain control with practical, neuro-affirming strategies.

The Biology Behind Emotional Dysregulation

Estrogen is far more than a reproductive hormone—it's a key player in brain function. One of its critical roles is modulating dopamine, the neurotransmitter responsible for focus, motivation, and emotional stability. For women with ADHD, whose brains already struggle with dopamine regulation, the drop in estrogen during perimenopause can feel like losing the last rung of a ladder.

Research shows that estrogen enhances dopamine receptor sensitivity and production. When estrogen levels decline, so does dopamine availability. This double deficit explains why ADHD symptoms like forgetfulness, emotional volatility, and brain fog intensify during perimenopause. Many women describe feeling like their brain has "glitched," leading to fears of early dementia. Understanding this biological cascade is the first step in reframing your experience: you're not broken. Your brain is adapting to a seismic shift.

Identifying Your Emotional Triggers

Self-awareness is your most powerful tool. Start by tracking emotional patterns alongside your menstrual cycle (even if it's irregular). Note days when frustration feels unmanageable or tears come unexpectedly. Common triggers include sensory overload (e.g., noisy environments), task overwhelm, or perceived criticism—all of which are harder to filter when dopamine is low.

For example, Sarah, a 42-year-old graphic designer, noticed her temper flared during client meetings scheduled in the late afternoon. Tracking revealed this was when her energy and focus were lowest. By shifting meetings to mornings and preparing with grounding techniques, she reduced her emotional reactivity.

Keep a simple journal or use apps like Daylio to log mood shifts alongside physical symptoms. Over time, patterns will emerge, helping you anticipate and mitigate triggers before they escalate.

Practical Techniques for Emotional Management

When emotions feel like a tidal wave, grounding strategies can anchor you. Mindfulness doesn't require meditation (though it helps)—it can be as simple as the "5-4-3-2-1" technique: Name five things you see, four you can touch, three you hear, two you smell, and one you taste. This forces your brain to shift from emotional reactivity to sensory awareness.

Cognitive-behavioral strategies are also invaluable. When overwhelmed, ask: "Is this emotion proportional to the event?" Often, hormonal shifts amplify reactions. Label the emotion ("I'm feeling rage, but this is a minor inconvenience") to create distance.

For ADHD-specific challenges, try "body doubling"—working alongside someone else, even virtually, to sustain motivation. Visual aids like color-coded calendars or sticky-note reminders can offset memory lapses. Remember, productivity hacks aren't one-size-fits-all. Experiment to find what works for your brain.

Building Your Support System

Isolation magnifies emotional struggles. Start by educating your inner circle. Explain that perimenopause and ADHD create unique hurdles, and you're developing tools to manage them. Frame requests concretely: "I need quiet time after work to decompress" or "Can we divide household tasks based on energy levels?"

Therapy, particularly with providers versed in ADHD and women's health, can be transformative. Online communities (like Perimenopause Hub or ADHD Reddit groups) offer validation and practical advice. Don't underestimate peer support—connecting with others who "get it" reduces shame.

Leveraging Resources

Beyond therapy and community, explore tools tailored to hormonal and neurological shifts. Apps like Clue or Flo track cycles and symptoms, helping predict rough patches. Nutritional interventions—like prioritizing protein for dopamine synthesis—can stabilize mood. Some women benefit from hormone replacement therapy (HRT); consult a menopause-literate doctor to discuss options.

Books like The ADHD Effect on Marriage or The Menopause Manifesto provide deeper dives into specific challenges. Podcasts (e.g., ADHD for Smart Ass Women) blend humor with actionable tips.

Perimenopause and ADHD can feel like a relentless tag-team, but knowledge dismantles fear. By understanding the biology, identifying triggers, and deploying targeted strategies, you can navigate this phase with resilience. Emotional dysregulation isn't a life sentence—it's a signal to adapt. You've survived every hard day so far. With the right tools, you'll not only survive but reclaim a sense of control. The crash is temporary. Your strength isn't.

9

Advanced Strategies for Severe Symptoms

For many women navigating the intersection of ADHD and perimenopause, the initial strategies—like organizing routines, mindfulness practices, and dietary adjustments—can provide meaningful relief. But there are times when these foundational tools simply aren't enough. When memory lapses become more frequent, emotional dysregulation feels overwhelming, and executive dysfunction disrupts daily life, it's a clear sign that more advanced interventions are necessary. This chapter is designed to guide you through these next steps, offering a roadmap of professional therapies, cutting-edge treatments, and innovative technologies to help you regain control and thrive during this challenging phase of life.

Setting the Stage: Recognizing Severe Symptoms

Severe ADHD symptoms during perimenopause can feel like a sudden and alarming decline in cognitive and emotional functioning. You might find yourself walking into a room only to forget why you're there, struggling to complete tasks that once felt manageable, or experiencing intense mood swings that leave you feeling out of control. These symptoms often overlap with the effects of estrogen decline, which directly impacts dopamine regulation—a neurotransmitter critical for focus, motivation, and emotional stability.

It's important to recognize that severe symptoms don't mean you're failing or that your earlier efforts were in vain. Rather, they signal a need for more comprehensive support. If basic strategies like using planners, setting reminders, or practicing mindfulness no longer provide sufficient relief, it's time to explore advanced approaches. Understanding the severity of your symptoms is the first step toward seeking the help you need to manage them effectively.

Professional Interventions: Finding Expert Help

When severe ADHD symptoms persist, seeking professional guidance becomes essential. Therapists, psychiatrists, and other healthcare providers can offer tailored interventions that address both ADHD and the hormonal changes of perimenopause. Cognitive Behavioral Therapy (CBT) is one of the most effective therapies for ADHD, helping you reframe negative thought patterns and develop practical strategies for managing inattention and impulsivity. Similarly, Dialectical Behavior Therapy (DBT) can be particularly helpful for emotional dysregulation, teaching skills like distress tolerance and emotional regulation.

Medication management is another critical component of professional care. Stimulant medications, commonly prescribed for ADHD, can help restore dopamine levels and improve focus. However, their effectiveness may vary as estrogen levels fluctuate. Collaborating with a knowledgeable psychiatrist who understands the interplay between ADHD and perimenopause can ensure your medication plan is optimized for your needs.

Hormone Replacement Therapy (HRT) is a game-changer for many women experiencing severe perimenopausal symptoms. By replenishing estrogen levels, HRT can indirectly support dopamine regulation, alleviating ADHD symptoms like brain fog and emotional instability.

However, HRT is not without risks, and it's essential to discuss its potential benefits and drawbacks with a healthcare provider who specializes in hormonal health.

Advanced Therapies: Neurofeedback and Beyond

For those seeking cutting-edge solutions, therapies like neurofeedback, Transcranial Magnetic Stimulation (TMS), and Mindfulness-Based Stress Reduction (MBSR) offer promising results. Neurofeedback is a non-invasive technique that trains your brain to regulate its activity more effectively. By monitoring brainwaves in real-time, neurofeedback sessions can help improve focus, reduce impulsivity, and enhance emotional stability. This therapy is particularly beneficial for women whose ADHD symptoms are exacerbated by hormonal changes.

Transcranial Magnetic Stimulation (TMS) is another innovative therapy that uses magnetic fields to stimulate specific areas of the brain. While traditionally used for depression, emerging research suggests that TMS may also benefit ADHD symptoms by enhancing neural connectivity and dopamine production. Though still relatively new, TMS offers a non-pharmacological option for those seeking alternative treatments.

Mindfulness-Based Stress Reduction (MBSR) combines mindfulness meditation with yoga and body awareness exercises. For women navigating the dual challenges of ADHD and perimenopause, MBSR can reduce stress, improve emotional regulation, and enhance overall well-being. Its focus on present-moment awareness can also help mitigate the mental clutter and overwhelm often associated with ADHD.

Technology-Driven Solutions: Tools for Empowerment

In our digital age, technology offers powerful tools for managing ADHD symptoms. Digital health apps like Todoist, Trello, and Habitica can help you stay organized, set reminders, and track your progress on tasks. These apps are especially useful for managing executive dysfunction, providing visual cues and gamified incentives to keep you motivated.

Wearable devices like smartwatches and fitness trackers can also play a role in managing ADHD. By monitoring physiological signals such as heart rate and sleep patterns, these devices offer insights into your body's stress levels and overall health. For example, noticing spikes in heart rate during stressful moments can prompt you to pause and practice a grounding technique.

AI-driven platforms take personalization to the next level, offering real-time behavioral insights and tailored recommendations. Apps like Brainwave or Luminosity analyze your cognitive patterns and suggest exercises to improve focus and memory. These technologies empower you to take charge of your symptoms by providing actionable data and feedback.

Building a Personalized Action Plan

Creating a personalized action plan is key to managing severe ADHD symptoms during perimenopause. Start by identifying your specific challenges—whether it's memory lapses, emotional dysregulation, or difficulty focusing. Then, explore the professional interventions, advanced therapies, and technological tools that align with your needs. For example, you might combine CBT sessions with neurofeedback training, supplement HRT with mindfulness practices, or use a digital health app alongside TMS therapy.

Regular monitoring is crucial to ensuring your plan remains effective. Keep a journal to track your symptoms, progress, and any changes in your mood or cognitive function. This will help you and your healthcare provider make informed adjustments to your treatment plan. Remember, there's no one-size-fits-all solution; the goal is to find the combination of strategies that works best for you.

Navigating severe ADHD symptoms during perimenopause can feel overwhelming, but it's important to remember that you're not alone—and help is available. By recognizing the limitations of basic strategies and exploring advanced interventions, you can take meaningful steps toward reclaiming your focus, emotional stability, and overall well-being. Whether it's through professional therapies like CBT and HRT, cutting-edge treatments like neurofeedback and TMS, or innovative technologies like digital health apps and wearable devices, a personalized approach can make all the difference. With the right tools and support, you can navigate this challenging phase of life with confidence and resilience.

10

Avoiding Common Pitfalls

As women in their 30s and 40s navigate the dual challenges of ADHD and perimenopause, they often find themselves grappling with intensified symptoms that can feel overwhelming. Brain fog, forgetfulness, and emotional dysregulation become more pronounced, leading many to fear the onset of early dementia. However, what they are often experiencing is a "crash" triggered by the interplay between fluctuating estrogen levels and dopamine regulation. This chapter delves into understanding this connection, identifying common mistakes, and offering practical strategies to maintain consistency and manage symptoms effectively. By learning from others' experiences and implementing advanced techniques, readers can anticipate and mitigate these cognitive challenges.

Understanding the Estrogen-Dopamine Connection

To comprehend why perimenopausal women with ADHD experience heightened symptoms, it's essential to explore the biological relationship between estrogen and dopamine. Estrogen plays a crucial role in modulating dopamine levels in the brain. Dopamine, a neurotransmitter associated with focus, motivation, and reward processing, is already dysregulated in individuals with ADHD. When estrogen levels drop during perimenopause, dopamine production and regulation are further compromised, exacerbating ADHD symptoms.

Recent research highlights this connection, emphasizing the need for hormonal awareness in managing ADHD during this life stage. Practical tips for monitoring hormonal changes include keeping a menstrual cycle tracker, noting mood and cognitive fluctuations, and consulting healthcare providers for personalized advice. By understanding this interplay, women can better anticipate and address their symptoms.

Common Mistakes Women Make

Several recurring mistakes can worsen ADHD symptoms during perimenopause. Neglecting to track hormonal changes is a significant oversight, as it prevents women from identifying patterns and preparing for cognitive crashes. Failing to adjust daily routines to accommodate energy and focus variations is another common error. Many women also overlook the importance of self-care, neglecting sleep, nutrition, and stress management, which are vital for hormonal balance and cognitive function.

Real-life examples illustrate these pitfalls. For instance, Sarah, a 42-year-old marketing executive, noticed her ADHD symptoms worsening but didn't link them to her irregular menstrual cycles. By the time she sought help, her work performance had significantly declined. Conversely, Maria, a 38-year-old teacher, proactively tracked her cycles and adjusted her schedule to include more rest during low-energy phases, mitigating her symptoms effectively.

Staying Consistent: Practical Strategies

Maintaining consistency is crucial for managing ADHD symptoms during perimenopause. Neuro-affirming productivity techniques can be particularly effective. Visual aids, such as color-coded calendars and checklists, help keep track of tasks and deadlines. Body doubling, where a companion works alongside you, can enhance focus and accountability. Breaking tasks into smaller, manageable steps prevents overwhelm and ensures steady progress.

Integrating these strategies into everyday life requires intentionality. Setting specific daily rituals, such as morning routines or wind-down practices, creates structure. Prioritizing tasks based on energy levels and hormonal cycles ensures that critical activities align with peak cognitive function. Regularly reviewing and adjusting these strategies based on changing needs fosters long-term consistency.

Learning from Others: Case Studies and Success Stories

Insights from case studies and success stories provide valuable lessons for managing ADHD during perimenopause. Emily, a 45-year-old entrepreneur, found that journaling helped her track mood and cognitive patterns, allowing her to anticipate and prepare for difficult days. She also built a support network of friends and colleagues who understood her challenges, providing encouragement and practical assistance.

Rachel, a 40-year-old artist, struggled with emotional dysregulation until she incorporated mindfulness practices into her routine. Meditation and deep-breathing exercises helped her manage stress and improve emotional stability. These stories underscore the importance of self-awareness, adaptability, and community in navigating ADHD symptoms during perimenopause.

Advanced Strategies for Long-term Management

For sustained management of ADHD symptoms during perimenopause, more advanced techniques are necessary. Building a robust support network, including healthcare providers, therapists, and peers, ensures comprehensive care. Utilizing technology, such as apps for task management and hormonal tracking, enhances organization and awareness.

Continuously adapting strategies to changing hormonal levels is crucial. Regular consultations with healthcare providers can help adjust treatment plans, including medication and lifestyle interventions. Incorporating holistic practices, such as yoga, acupuncture, and dietary changes, supports overall well-being and hormonal balance.

Navigating ADHD symptoms during perimenopause presents unique challenges, but understanding the estrogen-dopamine connection and avoiding common pitfalls can significantly mitigate these issues. By implementing practical strategies, learning from others' experiences, and adopting advanced techniques, women can manage their symptoms effectively and maintain consistency in their daily lives. This chapter provides a roadmap for anticipating and addressing cognitive crashes, empowering readers to take control of their well-being during this transformative life stage. With awareness, adaptability, and support, managing ADHD during perimenopause becomes a manageable and even empowering journey.

11

Building a Support Network

Navigating ADHD during perimenopause can feel like trying to find your way through a dense fog. The hormonal shifts of this life stage exacerbate ADHD symptoms, leaving many women feeling overwhelmed, misunderstood, and isolated. But you don't have to face this challenge alone. Building a support network—a circle of people who understand, validate, and assist you—can make all the difference.

This chapter explores why a support network is essential, how to identify and engage supportive individuals, and the unique benefits of peer support groups and online communities. Through practical strategies and real-life examples, you'll learn how to create a personalized support system that helps you manage ADHD symptoms during perimenopause with greater confidence and resilience.

Why a Support Network is Essential

The intersection of ADHD and perimenopause is a perfect storm. Estrogen, which plays a key role in regulating dopamine, declines during perimenopause. Since dopamine is already lower in individuals with ADHD, this hormonal shift can intensify symptoms like brain fog, forgetfulness, and emotional dysregulation. Many women describe feeling like they're "falling apart" or "losing their minds."

A support network provides emotional, practical, and cognitive assistance during this challenging time. Emotionally, supportive people can offer validation and reassurance when you're feeling overwhelmed. Practically, they can help with tasks that feel insurmountable, like organizing your schedule or remembering appointments. Cognitively, they can serve as a sounding board, helping you process decisions and problem-solve.

Take, for example, Sarah, a 42-year-old graphic designer who was recently diagnosed with ADHD. As she entered perimenopause, she noticed her ADHD symptoms becoming unmanageable. Her partner began helping her set reminders and organize her workspace, while a close friend offered a listening ear when Sarah felt frustrated. "Having people who understand and don't judge me has been a lifeline," Sarah shared.

Research supports the importance of social support for managing ADHD. Studies show that individuals with strong support systems experience lower levels of stress and better overall mental health. For women navigating perimenopause, this support can be transformative.

Identifying Potential Support Sources

Building a support network begins with identifying potential sources of support. These can include family members, friends, colleagues, and mental health professionals. But not everyone in your life will be equally understanding or supportive. Use the following checklist to evaluate potential support sources:

- Do they listen without judgment?
- Are they willing to learn about ADHD and perimenopause?
- Can they offer practical help when needed?
- Do they respect your boundaries?

Start by considering people who have shown empathy and reliability in the past. For example, a sibling who has always been a good listener or a colleague who is organized and detail-oriented might be good candidates.

Once you've identified potential supporters, approach them with honesty and clarity. Explain how ADHD and perimenopause are affecting you and what kind of support you're seeking. For instance, you might say, "I'm going through a tough time with my ADHD symptoms right now, and I'd really appreciate your help with [specific task or need]."

Engaging Support: Communication and Boundaries

Effective communication is key to engaging support. Start by articulating your needs clearly and specifically. Instead of saying, "I need help," try something like, "Could you help me brainstorm ways to stay on top of my deadlines?" or "Would you be willing to check in with me once a week to see how I'm doing?"

Setting boundaries is equally important. Let your supporters know what kind of help you're comfortable with and where you need space. For example, you might say, "I appreciate your advice, but sometimes I just need someone to listen without offering solutions."

It's also important to recognize that not everyone will understand your experience—and that's okay. Focus on nurturing relationships with those who are willing to learn and adapt. Over time, these connections can become a cornerstone of your support network.

Leveraging Peer Support Groups and Online Communities

One of the most powerful sources of support comes from connecting with others who share your experiences. Peer support groups and online communities offer a space where you can share challenges, exchange advice, and feel understood.

There's something uniquely comforting about talking to someone who truly "gets it." Whether it's swapping tips for managing brain fog or venting about the frustrations of forgetfulness, these groups provide validation and camaraderie.

Finding the right group is key. Look for organizations or forums specializing in ADHD, perimenopause, or both. Many groups offer both in-person and virtual options, making it easier to find a fit that works for you.

Case in point: Maria, a 38-year-old teacher, joined an online ADHD support group after struggling to cope with her worsening symptoms. Through the group, she discovered practical strategies for managing her workload and found a sense of belonging she hadn't experienced before. "It's like having a team of cheerleaders who also happen to understand exactly what you're going through," Maria said.

Case Studies of Successful Support Networks

Real-life examples can illustrate the transformative power of a support network. Consider the following case studies:

Emily, a 45-year-old marketing manager, felt isolated in her struggles with ADHD and perimenopause. She reached out to a therapist specializing in ADHD, who helped her develop coping strategies and connected her with a local support group. Emily also enlisted her husband's help with household tasks, freeing up mental energy for her work.

"Having a support system has made me feel less alone and more capable," she shared.

Similarly, Rachel, a 40-year-old writer, leaned on her close friends and family when her ADHD symptoms became overwhelming. She also joined an online community for women with ADHD, where she found encouragement and practical advice. "Knowing I'm not alone has given me the courage to keep going," Rachel said.

These stories highlight the importance of tailoring your support network to your unique needs and circumstances.

Maintaining and Evolving Your Support Network

A support network isn't static—it requires ongoing maintenance and adaptation. Schedule regular check-ins with your supporters to ensure the relationship remains balanced and mutually beneficial. Express gratitude for their help and recognize when their support makes a positive impact.

As your needs change, so too might your support network. For example, you might find that you need more help managing household tasks during particularly stressful periods or that you're ready to take on more responsibilities as your symptoms improve. Be open to evolving your network to reflect these shifts.

If you find yourself needing additional support, don't hesitate to seek it out. This might mean joining a new support group, consulting a different mental health professional, or reaching out to a trusted mentor.

Navigating ADHD during perimenopause is undoubtedly challenging, but you don't have to do it alone. Building a support network can provide the emotional, practical, and cognitive assistance you need to manage your symptoms and thrive.

By identifying supportive individuals, communicating your needs effectively, and leveraging peer support groups, you can create a network that empowers you to face this life stage with resilience and grace. Remember, support is not a sign of weakness—it's a testament to your strength and resourcefulness.

Take the first step today. Reach out to a trusted friend, explore a support group, or schedule a conversation with a mental health professional. You deserve the support and connection that can make this journey a little easier.

12

Maintaining Long-Term Success

For women with ADHD navigating perimenopause, the journey often feels like walking through a maze with shifting walls. Just when you think you've found a rhythm, hormonal fluctuations throw you off balance again. The key to long-term success isn't about finding a one-size-fits-all solution but building a flexible, adaptive system that works with your brain and body. This chapter is your guide to creating that system—one that accounts for the unpredictability of perimenopause while honoring the unique wiring of your ADHD brain.

Building a Sustainable Management Plan

The first step toward lasting success is developing a management plan that acknowledges both your ADHD and the hormonal changes of perimenopause. This isn't about rigid rules but about creating a framework that can bend without breaking. Start by identifying your personal triggers. For many women, certain times of the month—when estrogen levels dip—bring heightened brain fog, forgetfulness, or emotional volatility. Tracking these patterns is crucial.

Use a simple journal or app to log daily symptoms alongside your menstrual cycle (if you still have one) or other hormonal markers. Over time, you'll spot trends, like increased distractibility in the week before your period or heightened irritability during ovulation. Once you recognize these patterns, you can plan around them. For example, if you know focus will be shaky on certain days, schedule high-concentration tasks for your "better" times and save administrative or repetitive tasks for your lower-energy phases.

Neuro-affirming strategies are your allies here. Visual aids like color-coded calendars or sticky notes can compensate for memory lapses. Body doubling—working alongside someone else, even virtually—can boost accountability on days when motivation is scarce. Time-blocking, broken into short, manageable chunks, helps prevent overwhelm. The goal isn't perfection but predictability: knowing what's coming and having tools ready to meet it.

Adapting to Hormonal Changes

Understanding the science behind hormonal fluctuations can demystify much of what you're experiencing. Estrogen plays a critical role in dopamine regulation, and as it declines during perimenopause, ADHD symptoms often intensify. This isn't a personal failing; it's biology. But knowing this allows you to adapt.

One practical strategy is adjusting medication timing in consultation with your healthcare provider. Some women find their ADHD medication less effective during low-estrogen phases and benefit from slight dosage adjustments or splitting doses. Others explore hormone-supportive supplements like omega-3s, magnesium, or vitamin B6, which may help stabilize mood and cognition. Always discuss these options with a professional to ensure they align with your health profile.

Lifestyle changes can also buffer the impact of hormonal shifts. Regular exercise, particularly strength training and yoga, has been shown to support dopamine production and reduce stress. A protein-rich diet with steady blood sugar levels can prevent energy crashes that exacerbate brain fog. Prioritizing sleep is non-negotiable; even slight sleep deprivation worsens ADHD symptoms and hormonal imbalances.

Real-world examples bring these strategies to life. Take Maria, a 42-year-old graphic designer who noticed her ADHD symptoms spiked wildly during perimenopause. By tracking her cycle, she realized her worst days coincided with estrogen dips. She began scheduling creative work during her high-energy phases and used voice memos to capture ideas when focus waned. Small tweaks, like a protein-heavy breakfast and a midday walk, made a noticeable difference in her stability.

Celebrating Progress and Building Resilience

In the whirlwind of managing symptoms, it's easy to overlook progress. Yet celebrating small wins is a powerful tool for maintaining motivation. ADHD brains thrive on positive reinforcement, and perimenopause can make it harder to recognize your own achievements. Start by setting realistic, incremental goals. Instead of "I'll organize the entire house," try "I'll declutter one drawer today." Each completed task is a victory.

Create a visible progress tracker—a checklist, a jar of accomplishments, or a notes app where you jot down daily wins. These don't have to be monumental. "Remembered to take my medication" or "Took a five-minute break instead of pushing through burnout" counts. Over time, this record becomes a testament to your resilience, especially on days when self-doubt creeps in.

Case studies highlight the power of this approach. Lisa, a project manager, felt defeated when perimenopause amplified her forgetfulness. She started a "win log" and was surprised to see how often she problem-solved on the fly or asked for help instead of struggling alone. These moments, previously invisible to her, became proof of her adaptability.

Avoiding Common Pitfalls

Even with the best strategies, pitfalls await. One of the biggest is over-reliance on caffeine to combat fatigue. While it offers a quick boost, it can disrupt sleep and exacerbate anxiety, creating a vicious cycle. Instead of multiple coffees, try matcha for sustained energy or herbal teas for calming focus.

Neglecting self-care is another trap. When time feels scarce, women often sacrifice sleep, meals, or relaxation to meet demands. But perimenopause demands the opposite: more rest, more nourishment, more grace. Schedule self-care as you would a work meeting—non-negotiable and non-negotiable.

Losing perspective on progress is equally dangerous. ADHD brains tend to focus on what's unfinished, overlooking what's been achieved. Combat this by reviewing your progress tracker regularly or sharing wins with a trusted friend. Self-compassion is your anchor. On hard days, remind yourself: you're managing two significant physiological shifts at once. That's no small feat.

Long-term success with ADHD and perimenopause isn't about eliminating challenges but learning to navigate them with flexibility and self-awareness. By building a sustainable management plan, adapting to hormonal changes, celebrating progress, and avoiding common pitfalls, you transform chaos into a system that works for you.

Remember, this isn't a linear journey. Some days will feel like breakthroughs; others will require you to regroup. Both are part of the process. The goal isn't perfection—it's resilience. With the right tools and mindset, you can thrive through this transition, turning what once felt like a crash into a controlled, confident landing.